WILLOWS, WOMEN, HIGHWAYS AND THE SEA

JOHN FINCH

John Finch

WILLOWS, WOMEN, HIGHWAYS AND THE SEA
A Book of Poems

featuring ...

Song of the Corona Borealis
A Pocket Epic

A Selection of Works by a Young Poet

M.A.M. PUBLISHING

Copyright © 2006-2014 by John Finch. All rights reserved. Printed in the United States of America. No part of this book may be used or reproduced in any matter whatsoever without written permission except in the case of brief quotations listed in critical articles and reviews.

Second Edition

The characters and happenings in this book are entirely fictional. Any likeness to people, places, things and happenings, living, dead or inanimate, is purely coincidental.

ISBN 10: 099123880X

ISBN 13: 978-0-9912388-0-4

MAGNUS ATROX MUSA PUBLISHING
S.L.C. UT U.S.A.

To E.

CONTENTS

Second Edition Preface   x
Preface   xii

Youth

A Lifetime Past   1
Our Willow   2
Memoirs   6
Cry Forth!   7
Beat   8
Lottery Tickets or Check Stubs   9
If Winter Ends   10
Burned Out Folk Singers   11
3 Haiku   12
If the Rain Stops   13
The Best Advice I Can Give   14
Like Alone   15
Happy Birthday Me (Aug. 9th)   16
C, for Conscience   18
I Left the Fan Running For You   19
Ghosts and the Lack of Sleep   20
Eloping   21
Afternoon Dream   22
The Speaker   23
Fourth Street Sunglasses   24
Good Morning Magpie   26
State Lines   27
Best Painting I Imagine   29

CONTENTS

Explorations

Reflecting, Editing	33
Midnight Bathing	34
Blossoms	35
Spring in Urbania	36
Ha Tran	37
October Leaves	38
Love is a Sketch	39
Kaleidoscope Dresses	40
Private Hell	41
Lucky Strikes	42
She Runs White	43
White Line Interstates	44
Nights Like These	45
The Fox and the Moon	47
Bus Stop, All Made Up	49
Sordid City	50
Tea Leaves the Lake	51
Dickinson Crescendo	52
Book Sad Day	53
Hope Will Find Us Holding Hands	54
Sad Wyoming Night	55
Hello Reno	56
Birds at Abandoned House	58
Old Bank Robbers	59
What Lead to the Wharf	60
The Cold Desert	62
While They Live	63

Holy Sadness

Love is Our Midwife	67
Valentine's Day Massacre	68
The Road	70
Rambling Jazz	71
Still Green	72
Flowers on Dresses, Flowers on Cement	73
Good Night Cat	74

CONTENTS

Good Morning	75
It Loops	76
Always Going	77
Or Idaho, then Desert	78
Forward	79
Picture Love	80
The Birds and the Bees	81
Reality Patchwork	82
Ginsberg	83
Holy Sadness	84
Maybe	85

Over Hills, Over Horizons

Aquí	89
Arnold and Hecht's Woman	90
whenifeelalive	91
Over Hills, Over Horizons	92
Man on Church Steps	93
Dishes	94
That Evening Moment	95
Remember	96
A Poor Note (And a Poor Poem)	98
Ariadne	99
Secret	100
How We'd Make It	102
Song of Sex	103
Psalms Cigarette	106
Sitting Dream in Library	107
First Full Moon of Winter	108
Night	109

CONTENTS

Songs of Seas and Circles

Nostalgic Reproduction	113
Variations on Afternoon	114
These States	116
Only Once	118
Maryland	119
Breath	120
That Season We Said We Were in Love	121
If We Were Sounds Not People	122
Your Breath (A Little Bird Told Me)	123
Entirely	124
Love	126
Spring Showers	127
Just Dreaming Again	128
Jazz Fragment (Bird)	129
Touch	130
Poem Bridge	131
Train Dream	132
Heavy Love	133
Gone	134
Heavy Love II	135
Could You Just Tell Her?	136
Jazz Chorus I	137
The High and Low Notes	138
Song of Sea and Circle	139
A Poem Concerning Jeff Who Died	140
University Haiku	141
Dionysus Mourning	142

Epilogue

Song of the Corona Borealis	147

SECOND EDITION PREFACE

I was in such a rush to get the first edition of Willows out last year that I made a lot of exceptions in regards to the product I had pictured in my mind. This second edition addresses those concerns, and I am very pleased to present it to you all.

***

This book features a selection from the first six years of my attempts at writing poetry. The sections are split accordingly, with each marking movement into a new year—the entirety presenting a loose narrative of transition, development, exploration and realization. The poems deal with the everyday, but in doing so explore the macrocosm of the external, as well as the microcosm within.

My hope is to explore existence and the rhythms and brief melodies we find in the every day, in the symphony of being alive—the sounds words make, the way they make the voice vibrate and the mind ring, is musical, and often times, the things we see contain words which write a tune. Basically—the things we see are beautiful, and often times the words we use to explain those things go together in a way that is rhythmic and melodic, filled with assonance and dissonance and all kinds of other beautiful nonsense.

But really, all that is just theory, and I feel it doesn't always shine through, or even have anything to do with, a particular poem. I try to not confine myself in approach, or even necessarily style (though arguably from that blossoms a style), for the poem is an idea or a moment captured, and while you could strain to connect that moment to an ideology or concept, most often if you don't strain, an ideology or concept comes forth, already contained in the poem.

It isn't often I think a poem through before I lay it down on page. It seems more like a movement itself, something that swells within, and eventually outpours from the pen to page. I believe that is something like William Wordsworth said, if I remember correct.

I can only write what I see, but what is more I can only put down what passes through me as a person. Like a camera lens perhaps—taking pictures and trying to capture not only a moment, but also a story, a thought, some enlightening thing that has been seen that will help one move through their lives in a way different, dare I say better, than they did before.

That is all any artist, any person, hopes to do really.

***

Enjoy,

John Finch

POET'S PREFACE

these poems are
a sad narrative
of lovers and
love—many
types of love—
the love in lovely
lays as well as
the love in elation
of spring mornings—
of seeing that
pretty girl with
her umbrella and
her blonde hair
and her beauty—
cold—love
of friends—of
people smiled to
on street corners—
of grinning dogs
with tired tongues
and lazy cats
lounging—

but most of all

these poems are of
the love known only
in one's love and
in one's loneliness ...

Enjoy.

John Finch
February 12, 2013
Salt Lake City

WILLOWS, WOMEN,
HIGHWAYS AND THE SEA

YOUTH

A Lifetime Past

Reaching
early morning, shading out the light
A few more inches of play in mid
afternoon
      Blinking,
             We'd walk deeper under the willow

Bees would swarm
      Wrap around us like
Presents at a birthday party, reception
      Of a wedding

      White lace falling like
      Snow drops from the high
           Branches of a willow
               weeping

Our Willow

I.
Hallee's spitting sunflower seeds off the back porch
Holding hands I look at her with shy eyes
She turns, brown hues glimmer as she smiles
Her new sundress is pretty as her face
Rays cast down by the sun make her pale skin glow
She has freckles on her shoulders

Flowers blooming on white fabric
It falls just at her knees
Once again, cream colored skin
It makes me blush
Gardens reflect her attire
Blooming wonderfully I am confused
For which is more beautiful
Flower or flower girl
The thoughts create a funny face
She giggles, like a song, and kisses my cheek

II.
I forgot at some point that this was love
We both did
Those freckles on her shoulder I would kiss
Knotted in sheets
I would deflower my beloved flower girl
We would smile and pant afterward
Not realizing what we had done

III.
(That was the year I started drinking)
She would find my window
Most nights around eleven
Faint kisses on my collarbone
Until she found me useless
Or I simply didn't wake
Some nights she would leave

Others I would wake to sobbing
Holding her I would attempt comfort
What I used to be
So I would make promises
She'd crawl out my window
I'd break them
(That was the year my mother left)

IV.
I started missing her father's back porch
Far in mountains
The land her family owned but never cultivated
We had a willow
Our willow
Under it was where she told me
She was leaving town
She was going to be somebody
The mountains, the tree, the houses
They were never enough for her

Thrift shops
The old and comfortable — the sure thing
Just bland and boring
She said she loved me
She said she'd write me everyday

V.
It started that way
I drank a lot that summer
She knew, and I knew she did
Her letters became more spaced
Shallow
Sorrowful

VI.
Then
I checked my mail every day
An entire month
Nothing

VII.
July — Nothing.

VIII.
August — Nothing.

IX.
September — Nothing.

X.
October —
I got a letter
Her writing was different now
The tone, the attitude
An apology
How busy she was!
How happy
I would love it there
The city
Beautiful buildings and people
Shops, so many, with beautiful things
From Paris, from London
Even from the East

Our thrift stores had burned down
Our town forgotten
I was just a faint memory
Something she couldn't quite let go of
Yet

XI.
I waited yet another month
It used to take a week
This letter I took out to the willow
Our willow
I read it there, some of the branches were missing
Trees and people die
I watched the tree die that day
Because its heart was split in two

XII.
The letter read,
"I said I loved you,
And I did. We were young
things don't last forever."
We had grown too far apart
There was another greater than me

They were married
A year later
I heard she was beautiful
She walked off the back porch
To the alter in her father's back yard
I didn't attend
My invitation was burnt

XIII.
I lived in that town
Working
Although it came second to my drinking
My father always shook his head
But strangely understood
We had both lost our women
I hadn't seen my mother in five years
The city had swallowed them

XIV.
I met a girl by the name of Anne
She had blonde hair
Green eyes and very peach skin
It always managed to tangle itself in my sheets
Yes, she was beautiful
She put up with me
Her sad eyes knew she was trapped in the town
With the thrift shops and the dead willows
Our willow
She'd cry at night
I'd lay with her and occasionally call her
Hallee
She'd pretend she didn't notice

Memoirs

City lights flickering
Dimly lit streets flowing below sunspotted buildings
Acid burns holes in rooftops
Trickling and slowly decaying a life's work
The water warping the memoirs
Unattended stationary, stationary on the desk
Ink spills
A picture emerges from the mess
No longer words
The life is an image.

Cry Forth!

Where are the Zen lunatics?
The bohemian philosophers?
The mad writers?
The worry free lovers?
The high poets?
The crazed messengers?
Where are our fathers?
Our friends?
Our soul mates?

I call to you, modern saints!
I call to you, avid searchers!
I call to you, Truth!

Beat

Mad jazz singers blaring,
the gathered dance and bop
Tossing ladies between their legs,
hair slicked back and eyes shimmering
Chicks with ringlets catch attention—
Digging them and hoping for later rendezvous

Down hallway kick slick shoes
pantry doors banging shut
ringing like the trumpet singing
out like the caw-filled crow
Dance, red dress masquerade and
smile, lit cigarette—rest now
on painted lips

Lottery Tickets or Check Stubs

there is no promise
you have to trust in what I know
and only I know
I've never made you stay
nor will I ever, this isn't the life
at least for the doubters
the ones that need action
besides smoke filled rooms
and half bottles of whiskey
broken typewriters and the tapping
of keys echoing across empty
unfurnished places
Yeah, this isn't the life
for promises, but is one
for nonsensical love making
and fool hearty lovers —

So you have a choice
you can play the tracks and the
lottery, hoping for lucky sevens.
or you can go out and find another,
someone who is more paycheck,
more of a best bet,
backup plan
type of fellow

If Winter Ends

the cat, claws outstretched
little voice penetrating through
the unfurnished room
waiting for
absolute departure from the exs
and a new life in a new
city with a new cat and a
new woman
god, she's beautiful
and you can't deny she moves and
feels and trembles like the willow
swaying in the backyard I left
behind the old house I abandoned
a couple years ago
I wouldn't have thought
in new basement apartments
I'd be sober
and unalone for once
with wedding bands taken by
surprise in the shower
where the fog laces mirror
and the reflection staring back
actually has eyes that aren't sunken in
and aren't surrounded by yellow
like urine in the middle of snow angels
where did all the snow go?
frozen in mid-July and disappearing
as the cat bats the stocking cap from
the top of my head
I can't help but think
maybe winter was longer than expected
but maybe the chill miserable nights
were worth it

Burned Out Folk Singers

exhausted, like your act, like your life
it's tired, you're tired, you mirror me
perfect reflection and though you disappoint
I love you for it, doesn't make sense,
thanking you, for tonight I remembered I was
in love, I fell out of love soon after
freedom, how perfect, how sorrowful
me and you are deadly,
deathly,
just give us a fifth and we'll
tear this town
apart

3 Haiku

Cascading blossom
Oh beautiful! Straight flax crown
A queen amongst us

A single branch
Stretches to touch the pumpkin patch
Only weeks from harvest

A magpie lands
Between two pines in snow fall
Essence of black and white

If the Rain Stops

you wonder at night
while the rain beads down
on chipping window sills
if the water will stop falling
if perhaps the flowers
will dry up and wither
and if the people are
like flowers,
are like
flowers
and like flowers
will they wither
and decay if the
rain stops and the
tapping on the window-
sill stops
and if the long haired girl
stops
playing by the side of
shores and if,
when the rain stops,
if
peace
will follow

The Best Advice I Can Give

Write poetry
for only yourself
for no other eyes
and nail it to your wall
let that nail collect
and smile
because you know yourself

Like Alone

silence
taking deep breathes
that should echo across the room
but your figure remains
like still life photography
and your breath
stays perfectly
in place
in reflection of your body

I get motion sick
from lack
of movement
to focus on
and like the beginning
it is frightening
but now not from tension
sorrow drapes down
from corners in the room
and you disappear
into darkness
and I lay
alone

like it used to be

Happy Birthday Me (Aug. 9th)

past moments creeping up
in envelope familiar embrace as smiling faces
gather around the dinner table to discuss and to
play the roles of the parts we've been addressed

still soaking wet with the night's tears
as heavens fall in delicate and sweeping patterns
beadlets dropping from hair to pant leg, shoulders to chest
so wet with smiles and the drinking of the night sky

as the cool breeze swims through apartment
the ceiling fan spinning drafts from walls and collapsing
the night embrace — the love of a new beginning
of the true new year, where I truly began my year, with light
filled eyes

flickering eyes reflecting candlelight
in dark room reflecting night, the sweet smell of wetting
pavement, moon curtains close their fair skin outstretch cross
the hardwood floor slightly swaying papers of past work
on the desk — the wind

sifting through shining treasures and words and words from
fingertips, from ink stained, smeared book pages, notebooks,
blank white sheets, stacks of pens and drawers of more —
water staining thirsting desk top

from city to city, coast, cloud yawning
into the open night we walk and sing
leaving the umbrella in the house
gathering around the licorice smoke
wisping lovingly with the open air
as words continue to float up and up
with thoughts and dreams and
Love
as the light fades and the breeze sways
the candles wave to me goodbye — again I light them, the fire
it gently licks and lays, strength quivering, amplifying,
all in single breath with the windows open still offering the
night — such blessing

as the trees once again sway outside
the wind sending messages through windowsill
while the water soaks and trickles down to roots, deep inside
the earth as I breathe my first new sigh of life, and pass softly
sleeping,
smiling
in the night ...

C, for Conscience

dark room
touching beauty
with the tips of fingers
seeing outlines
and the movement of her figure
soon beneath mine
my hand tugging
at her hair
a shade of lighter brown
unlike my other love
she moves different
her hips
touching mine
she is rounder
not a willow
fuller
a firmer touch
my teeth graze her neck
trembling
for guilt should consume
yet it stands quietly at the door
tapping foot lightly
awaiting my departure

I Left the Fan Running for You

I left the fan
running for you
I know the sound
helps lull you to sleep
because the sounds
of the outside
world around
are too distracting
too overwhelming
to allow you rest

you are gone but
I left the fan running
for you
it sits in the corner
blowing breezes
against the wall
of the basement apartment

I left the fan
running for you
in case
you decide to come home
at least what I believe
should be your home

I just want you to know
I left the fan running
for you
in case you decided
you were still
in love with me

Ghosts and Lack of Sleep

tired and taking
green pills with a mouthful
of saliva
too lazy to travel
downstairs to get a glass
of water or whatever
will help sleep come,
if it weren't for
ghosts and frightening
feelings creeping up
perking up
neck hairs
in the dark
I'd be fine,
tho I wonder
if they are in the room
or if their room is rented in my
mind
and if they exist,
or once existed
as past relationships,
acquaintances,
one night stands,
drinking buddies,
sadness
or all of the above

Eloping

it's spitting
the five digit postal code,
scribbled and jotted like
the cat sitting in corner,
quiet and silent and sparse,
hair is falling out,
each follicle following the draft
down on eyelashes,
the ceiling fan spewing
inane ramblings and
television set with visions
of romance still being alive
still being alive
romantics
still being alive
The dash – meaning
the new act of God
in wedding bands
and Christlike keepsakes
corner store pawn shops
counting down days in
blue markers on blue lined papers
eloping to the next room
and the next room over towards
the next state
a neon suicide
passed out apartment blazing saddles
in corner chairs I rest with hands outstretched
for the day when the ring falls
in about a week
the ring falls –
looking up at the ceiling fan
the ceiling fan cycle
wishing that cycle would end
and love would finally be made –
    we'd finally be made ...

Afternoon Dream

I walk through
streets barefoot
in smiling reverence
to the swaying breeze

small white flowers grow on grass
I feel
hope still lingers

raindrop tears of summer
smiling with red flashes
the tree of love

the wind picks up
and girl moves
her body embraced
in two hoops,

I weep
as I love her

The Speaker

       Through darkened California streets
with soft leather shoes
the bottoms wearing — (They were brown
                          mine were black)
With matted hair caked on pale forehead
past shoulders, with an ever-long beard
scribbling poems between drags — High on tea in the park
      (As if Ginsberg was entrapped and twenty)
the sea breeze salting his lips, slightly chapped

Opening mouth on street corner —
lines and lines dancing among ears of the new beat,
     Young kids trying their best in a new age
the words increasing in quality as fierceness takes his throat,
       begins to crown

       The yellows and golds of his mane burn the mind
             loving-like lips begin to crack
    and
             he begins —

Fourth Street Sunglasses

Down 'cross town
there's a chick
with sunglasses on

she's jiving by
record player
jazz music — bop!
— Coltrane, "Blow baby!
Blow!"

– Blow cat blow!
For that lost little soul
in her chic skirt,
stocking feet dance floor

I'm on corner
of Fourth Street
— positively
mad sped hip lingo
pouring in breath
'tween cigarette smoke –
high cat story time

 – Blow cat! Blow!

That gone chick
still sock swaying,
tea high,
'tween horn blast
and thought,
thinking of
mad sped life
truth

Sweet record
alto background
fast slow,
bop, beedle dee dee dee dee bop

hardwood floor,
makeshift pillow, watching
gone girl
in sunglasses

Good Morning Magpie

as the bird circles round
eyes alight
skin shakes —
delight through body
only slight
fear of wild

pecking at rubbers
on shoes, stares
head cocks —
goosepimples rise
on skin
gazing at blacks

and whites
of magpie
circle fly about —
the three of us, simply
seated upon grass
watching
the morning leaves

State Lines

wonder– may I
if you drink tonight
does your wined stained lip
protrude ever so slightly
in that darling pout
as your raise your glass –

Do you cheer
to the following month
the end of the work day
– birth of the night

as tire treads
leave spaces in the grass
as the smokers huddle
near
the kitchen window
– a refuge from the cold

I sleep
should I dream?
of your safe arrival
as you pull your car in the drive
where I
could never park it straight
where you
were drunk and said you wanted to go to the river
– if we would have

– in the morning
as your eyes are slits
your hands are spiders
traversing
across the table
for a glass of water –
the shakes

– in my morning
could let you in
for coffee
if you wanted

Best Painting I Imagine

two pianos sit in the rain
laughing, in a white dress
you must be,
soaked, shivering, smiling —
as the rain falls
you dance with eyes alight,
your voice ringing
beautifully

EXPLORATIONS

Reflecting, Editing

dripping – the sink
in the kitchen
streaks water
on silver bowl
collecting
like sacrament,
tithing –

there's a pool
we'll baptize
and bastardize
as we run through
– midwinter, summer,
or spring
when you come
home,
holding hands –

ink
doesn't share warmth
– though
perhaps
brings it closer –
cutting lines
while you cut
classes
– black pens,
blackouts,
love

Midnight Bathing

I listen
to the woman
upstairs bathe
reading
on my couch
the water sways –

ripples
echo
from the floorboards
my mind echoes
curious –

nearly a year
she has lived
above
and
I've yet
to see her –

wonder
if her bath
is beautiful
as I
imagine

Blossoms

there are a million blossoms
they lay outside my window
the wind beds them to the ground
while the sun pulls them higher

I've seen a thousand blossoms
at least a hundred experienced
they smile and brown eyes shimmer
or perhaps they were blue
maybe green, hazel

they have bare shoulders under sunlight
that is always the same
they dance in circles and smile
you blush when you see them
after your season comes to end

there are very few blossoms
you can pick from the ground
with roots buried deep

which blossom
is the one which will
uproot for me

I wonder

Spring in Urbania

trees cast shadows
webbing concrete below,
falling leaves,
the last of autumn, as
green climbs into the sky
intermingling with the blues,
painting a picture of heaven
over rock divot
pathway unfurling
in front of footfall

flower blooms
in peripheral along siding
of banking institute
pitching shadow where
blossom should be radiant

worn leathers over warm
concrete billow pathway,
down dirty street,
around shadow-cast alley,
turn away instead stare at
matching stop sign,
same color as buds

sun shine smile
down radiate the beauty
walking toward
in short paisley dress,
grin to rival light fall
ing on pale face
sparkling spring

Ha Tran

there is a little Buddha who works in factory
his eyes shimmer when he smiles,
wrinkles appear on his face

his voice is small, urging,
fragile English with Vietnamese accent
he smiles and waves me to the back room

dark, strong coffee poured in plastic cup
brown bubbles dance where spout allows
he smiles, asking, 'Sugar? Sugar?'

the smile stands upon his face as he pours his own
stepping out to floor again
enlightenment in form

October Leaves

thoughts rekindle
rolling cigarettes
on Gideons Bible
(not in blasphemy,
it is the best fitting
book in one's lap)
as my mind falls back
fall, fall, falling, Fall —
as she was dolled up
along river bank
months have come and
past is always
steadfast in heart,
learning love
in new way,
deconstruction
of ego, simple dash
of knowledge
how she was beautiful
in half lit room
whispers
the one I love
she never said it back,
I'm afraid

Love is a Sketch

love
is actually a sketch,

the underlying
shape
of the textured painting,
not the painting itself

love
is actually a skeleton

like the ones
hidden in closets,
giving you depth
with structure

love
is actually your hand,

not in mine,
the shape, size, curvature,
the act of
waving goodbye

Kaleidoscope Dresses

coming home to
messages from
the woman with the red door
I lay on the floor
with a smile
finally

picking On the Road
out of San Francisco's hands
with a hug
goddamn her
looking so beautiful on
such a cloudy day

washing face
in speckled mirror
rose colored cheeks
rose colored glasses
still sitting
from last fall

roses blooming
the poetry
a mess
like passing reflections

Private Hell

I feel disappointing
smashing fists
on keyboard
drinking blur
sidewalk silhouette
cellphone pictures
subway glares
keyed cars
vomit alleyways
each person
just alone
in their
private hell

Lucky Strikes

she goes lightly
treading over dream
like a cloud lingering in sky
throwing up rainbows
making bile as wonderful
as snow trickling down throats
the drip
of rain patter windowsill
warping embrace
I feel she touches me
sometimes, though neither know
like lapping waves
sitting in another lap
as I sit on porch dragging
myself and this Lucky Strike
further down
he's going down
between her thighs
while I sit screaming
this basement will never fill
with enough noise
bring the boys home
bring me home
and I'll lay beside —
I've never been
so lucky …
Oh, I wish you'd fuck me …
just shut my eyes
love me
(or pretend
       'til this cigarette ends) …

She Runs White

I couldn't help it
in that garbage bag
dripping
yelling
"What else to do!
For tonight we'll scream love."
and you went on running through the rain
the lights
from the street lamps
and neon buildings
shimmered off the soaked cement
I could taste the grass
smell crawling through the
damp air
where your breath held still
like I had you in my arms
and you kept running
we sprung from roof top to roof top
never loosing footing
falling like the rain
stretching out my fingers
just to catch a glimpse
of your dress swaying with
that gorgeous movement ahead
you're a damn good runner
"Catch up, lover!"
you yelled it back
with that mock tone you use
the one when someone says fool things
I kept reaching
but the flower print slipped
flicking rain into my eyes—

White Line Interstates

I wonder how many gets us from here to there
the little white lines that scour the highway
a pale face in passing headlights – wide eyes
chain smoking cigarette, butts flicked out
into the night sky the stars go, climbing
follow this pavement trail – one love
to the next, until the next town and a new dress-
ed up in the finest suit – though, I know
I'll never be so pristine –
I'll keep trying, pulling levers on slot machines
smiling between cigarette drags,
another stop along the freeway, bathroom
stained wall graffiti, filling up the gas tank
sad eyed cashier trapped behind the register
what's new in the thrift store – the latest news
licking lips and closing car door
cigarette smoke still trailing from fingertips
then pallid lips – smile, that shape near perfect
rounded face and dimpled cheeks
we flick off the lights
in motel rooms, cheap tawdry, off the interstate –
on the interstate – more lines to pick us up in the morning
for a near six more hours between gas stations,
road locomotives and the blue sky spanning
more miles as you switch the disc
uptempo running around car doors as the wind
whistles through window
carry smoke far into the night – you smile
another passing headlight lets me know it –
you blush, content –
and the white lines continue

Nights Like These

coming home
sixteen hour work
bank statement mail box
hallway smell
foot on green
carpet
door open to apartment
too warm
oven smell burning
attempt
at dinner
empty couch
empty bowl
red eyes slit
face in sheet
I miss them

holding pillow in frail attempt
comforting
cradling
book in hand silent read –
once aloud – angels singing night
seeing sunrise
creep over as the Veil opens
due to your minds
entangling, open, with one
another – Us
walking over hardwood
eyes blazing
a million suns simply on the tips of tongues
wit, wisdom, happiness
love

darker now
as sun sets
cover over – head on blanket
boxes littering apartment
lovers in another state
lovers in the same state
lovers in my state
of mind – stating (more precisely –
screaming) love
from more than tongues or hearts
but souls

I miss them ...

The Fox and the Moon

the fox plays his flute
on a bench
beneath a willow

while the moon
she smiles
for miles and miles –

she's been away
a couple days
but still he plays –

sweet tunes
lacing melodies
in darkness

for the babes, ducks
floating on ponds
he peers over the fawns

the speckled backs
his tune
carries on –

as he awaits
dreaded dawn
his lover's face
sinking

with his heart
blessed
her sullen smirk
dissipating –

song of the lark
sun rising
dream until
her smile pleasing

good night moon
says he

and the flute carries her to bed ...

Bus Stop, All Made Up

started spitting and cursing
pitting verses profane -
please refrain -
the old woman's begging us, sitting at the bus stop
I got
a cigarette from my lips, cuffed sleeves
a hole in my sock
that you'll never see -
cop drives by and
eyes us -
as if the sky fell fingers
pointing – culprits, soon to be, without
a doubt -
doubting whether or not
we'll make it
down main, stumble stutter -
pish posh – punk rock anarchy
another day down the drain, the bottle drained
laughing in the rain,
who am I to say
that I could make you stay
heading away -
Californ – i – a
play, play, play –

Sordid City

watched kids
poking caterpillars
with stick on the front lawn
the grass green growing round
their bare feet
with the asphalt street
blaring in the corner -
heat off pavement
mailboxes —
man jumping batteries
in the driveway
cross the greenery
golf fairway
dreaming of city
far, far
away
today
breaking coffee cups
on marble counter tops
smoking cigarettes
cursing glass stuck in foot —
the words
head out window
past the turning leaves
and get gone

Tea Leaves the Lake

back
behind the shed
where the willow's o'erhead
there's a pond
we saw b'fore dawn -
where lake lights tingle
intermingling with stars -
across the river bank
you hear the brawlers
at the bars -
while we lay in embrace
tracing frown lines on your face -
displaced
disjunct time scape -
scraping the last of the resin
from the bowl,
both of us
overfull -
words spouting,
smoke crawling,
while you're pouting
the birds are crowing,
the sun is rising
our goodbyes and
promise
of another meet
again

Dickinson Crescendo

Tea leaves,
the lake dry,
the birds ahead,
up in the sky,
cats along
the fence's edge
lady in white
waits to be wed

so sits she
in little room
while flowers bloom,
lovers croon -
until the day
the friar say
she passed away...
Miss Emily

a gravestone reads
but does deceive
for you see
married was she
her loving groom – poetry
tut tut tut tut
tee hee hee hee

Book Sad Day

the television
static,
pink blue, white – cold images
the great wall of
bookshelves –
I am raging
on the inside,
smoking cigarettes outside

Hope Will Find Us Holding Hands

wake up to a smile,
thousand miles 'way,
could write another simile
of moon instead I lay
the sun overhead,
laying in my bed,
if this keeps repeating,
I'll be repenting

waking up to a smile
as you lay stretched out
beside
and you come along
for the ride
through forests
'til the tide,
'til you turn,
I cry —

a fire at the arcade,
where our wild beasts play

Sad Wyoming Night

pulling coats closer in the sleet-sheet night,
a fleeting glance kicked over the underpass
walking over soaked cement in sogged leathers
as cars pass fast below, hydro-
planing, slick, slide, a deep breath
sigh of relief - - ponies
tea high at the side of super markets
ducking under overhang in small town
Wyoming, wild west, the girl on front porch
whistling, her stomach showing, hustling,
it's a sad kind of night, another smoke
'fore turning 'round and kicking down
Dewar Drive, smiling, ducking into
dive bar, downtown, if there were such,
we're such...

Hello Reno

stuffing pennies into pockets
walking on worn leather
from casino to casino,
wide eyes, tea high,
cop on corner,
staring at the sky,
red carpet furling around corner
slot machine clicking,
the sound of change descending
hurry through,
sit at bar under bright neons,
finding myself
thinking
of whose shoulders
the world is sitting,
a man is sitting
on cement sidewalk holding sign saying,
"God bless."
thinking Nietzsche,
"God is dead."
holding words heavy
on deep spattered,
soaked in ink page
a man walks by smoking cigarette,
taking long drags and long steps
long legs,
a suit, fairly worn
I relate to him,

not because I'm smoking a cigarette too,
the smoke inhaling,
nicotine craving, day to day,
but a fellow human,
oh failing,
walking away
forgetting the fact
that we are all forgetting the fact,
a real class act,
next fellow in shined shoes,
his watch is shined,
he's got a shined belt buckle,
a man offers to shine his suit,
and all the tin men run on oil,
sitting in bathroom,
curling legs up to show no one,
pondering and trying to catch
a minute alone with you,
me,
a minute alone to fight the lonely,
going to sleep to
jazz records,
reading Time magazine every day,
today, had a better day,
and so the record plays

Birds at Abandoned House

abandoned house, down the street,
the corner of the avenue,
where the blue jays gather
hopping forked feet,
leaving imprints in the dirt,
for the lawn hasn't had a drink
in years
two doves, shuffling in front lawn
side by side,
chests white,
cooing

Old Bank Robbers

The street lamps flicker overhead
a car passing, headlights, snow falling
and tightly they tuck in their beds
they're hiding away from the Feds
though their eyelids are steadily lulling

The wife she was the driver
the husband he was the gun
she never felt more aliver
and he'd never had more fun

They followed them through town
sirens flashing red and blue
On the freeway, then around
Until the sun went down
and off in the distance they flew

Finally in a little town
they pulled off the winding road
decided to settle down
raise children and get old

What Lead to the Wharf

I never knew exactly what you were saying,
looking at me with big brown eyes,
undress, capture, spiral, swirl,
the wind is blowing round us
and the breeze is picking up your skirt.
My lungs hurt.
So we sit on park benches and you worry,
say I shouldn't smoke,
I get better for a while,
'til we drive out past salt flats,
holding hands and singing songs
to songs singing from the radio
and I just have to remember to breathe
I can see headlights up ahead,
a sea of beasts crawling on the back of the great beast,
black snake,
sifting over desert
as we climb Donnor Pass in middle of the night and my vision is doubled
and my mind is racing
while you're sleeping in the passenger seat,
I see it, the city, out in front of me,
you wake
over the Golden Gate,
we pay toll and pool our dollars over the great
pool of the Pacific Ocean,

the beach down below feet, down below tire treads,
we drive over it, wind blowing,
spend morning,
four o'clock check in,
sleeping,
waking up and laying next to you,
making love as sun
sifts through thin veiled window,
drinking wine after shower,
cleaned up,
watching you brush your hair,
wrapped in towel sitting at desk in room,
I look out over the ocean, blue swaying,
gulls overhead though pass from sight,
pants on,
smile from stained lips,
and you look beautiful as you always do,
walking out the front door
smiling drunk at woman at desk, sunglasses on
catching shuttle outside
before the city

The Cold Desert

falling down the mineshaft
watching sad girls,
overweight on stripper poles,
singing with sad souls,
songs that remind
of a time when we didn't have
a drink in hand
instead, with hands in hands,
happy, smiling – fun
without the stumble
and lack of function
clutching bottle
close,
rum and coke,
caught cold
walking through the cold
desert –
forgetting

While They Live

there's a man near the barrel –
and overhead –
chickens clucking, children chuckling
around his bed –
he is sleeping,
they've ceased their weeping,
simply playing
in the dirt

HOLY SADNESS

Love is Our Midwife

my mind sees cosmic vibrations
in coffee cups, at train stations,
the most sow-able plantation
awaiting fruition,
playing the flirtation
of death
decaying,
each day fading
in television ratings,
while the children playing,
hardly notice, ever pursuing
comic vibrations racing
through
vision
after
vision
through
death
after
death
through
life,
birthed by mid-wife
called
Love

Valentine's Day Massacre

We are the center of the universe
Ohm
CRASH PWWWW CRRRR
       the car is hit on the driver's side
       someone runs the red light
       the sound sings
a man runs away from the scene
pedestrians watch, slinking closely
feeding morbid curiosity

       TO LOOK AT DESTRUCTION AND BE MORE
HUMAN
like the rest of them
sitting in front of telescreens –
CARCUS
       I say on side of road
       as he picks up the phone and puts down the bad news
(could have been cut off from car crash –
       Only too perfect, only too likely...)
we time it perfectly
to walk back
with no sack
watching lady pulled from seat in stretcher
man walking sober line surrounded by cops
bulging eyes feeding at their troughs
       if I didn't see her mouth move we would have felt bad

I HATED EVERY SECOND OF THIS
take your car crash, take your empty sack,
take your worn leathers, take your universe,
       I will sit and dig my grave in the front lawn,
            and as was pointed out,
       I'd "just end up with a half dug grave
            and a whole lot of trouble."

WHY DID THEY TAKE AWAY MY RIGHT TO DIG MY OWN GRAVESITE

why did they take away my grave?
> the room flashes
> and his movement is spliced into photograph

FATALISM
> (a little pessimistic wouldn't you say?
> "They said, 'You'll be alright...' to comfort a dying woman...")

What can we do to make the world more fun?
BLOW IT UP

IN HIGH DEFINITION
television shrine
glaring, blaring,
blowing things up, killing things, crashing things, raping things
And I want to be the things
> FUCK YOU
> says the universe
> you can't be any of those things
> because you are the center of the universe

(the sound of an atom bomb)
Great glorious disappointment.
I have gone blind from visual stimulation
> and the lawn's still lacking holes.

The Road

There is no greaterer perfection
than each person's imperfection
laughing as I ponder this
walking down the road.

I wonder if you've gone somewhere
each person's placement here or there
everywhere the monks do sit
all along the road.

And if long do you ponder this
a slow rise of head above the mist
the path will open smiling
showing you the road.

Rambling Jazz

to Frisco
with trumpet blaring,
the old ambassador
sitting in hard shell,
saxophone singing,
staring at stars,
sounds
ocean

Still Green

yellow flower, line drawn crooked, big black smudge
    smeared over the canvas—
        always flaw in near-perfect

never mind it, sitting spun, peace in place
    of dream disorient—
        and so we go

it's in the laying, horrid lying, never meant no harm
    sorry, selfish, sad sack—
        apologize, good deed

I'm buried, buying tickets, burning prints
    of finger tips—
        still green behind the ears

after all these years

Flowers on Dresses, Flowers on Cement

always falling for flower dresses,
flowers falling on cement,
pulling tho pulled,
from pavement smiling,
pleasant moment,
changing pace

Goodnight Cat

I'm found walking down street
my head up in the clouds,
a church to my right,
my peripheral sight,
so I ponder saved,
and wonder
if I'm too far past it
for the past it
holds heavy,
I sigh heavy –
a black cat crosses
path, it
then darts from sight,
goodnight –
I say,
polite

Good Morning

this is your morning,
sun shining,
rolled cigarette smoking
between fingertips,
it's that first deep breath
rising your head
the sigh sound it makes,
messed hair
slighted eyes
and smile
looking up at
curled clouds –
you're awake,
good morning

It Loops

if you remember me,
was I anything
but a passing dream,
a tearing seam,
seemingly useless
as time passes
I wonder

Always Going

you were waves crashing
through the rocks
sifting the sand
reaching forward
sliding masses in the palm of your hand –
now
watching waves goodbye with sad eyes,
color of stoplights –
I am GO
I've always been going,
as you once were –
going,

always going

Or Idaho, then Desert

never meant much –
highway line, by-the-way line,
leaving in the morning,
the opposite way –
stretching thumbs out in the sun-light
golden hair lit up,
halos 'round their heads –
I'd cross myself if catholic,
start the car
pointed north –
heavy –
their packs must be
hunchbacked by the side of the road
and so it goes –
through the forks and waterfalls –
driving jackpot,
through the desert –
gas station attendant
chewing tobacco spit on
gas station pavement –
turn the key, turning face –

heading to the sunset,
setting over hillside
sitting in the distance

Forward

You can spend the whole night pondering
with the moon laying face down, staring –
you'll find you can't find the way back,
         because that isn't the way we go,
         but we continue with what we know.

Picture Love

I was asked to picture love today,
I pictured a vast abyss,
for love is nothingness,
the vacuum back to the eternal
eithos

The Birds and the Bees

pornographic lactation
flowing into the mouths of the children
from the thousand tits
on the great boob of Christ

someone must teach them of intercourse

let it be the internet

Reality Patchwork

why must my reality
puzzle, cut and piece into place
amongst all the others –
I am not a piece to place,
for in no place have I found peace –

this world is not my big picture –

mother, father,
your reality is
disappointing,
why must I blindly be
part of such –
I refuse
to use my energies to settle in the masses
to join the refuse
of great ideas –

I will be no part,
unless it be the Mover,
who of himself
is no part,
but a separate whole –

I will be no part,
unless it be the axis,
the mad light shining down
when the moon's made full.

Ginsberg

      Ah, silly sad saint, practiced poet of the eternal
bearded sophist, bearded solace, bearded
and holy
holey shoes, holey pants, walking down the holy road
with a smile shown –

your love left traced on sills of windows in early morning dews,
a breath from past, passing over worn wood,
white paint flaking down to dirt and dust below,
where the chickens pecked
before cement street gave farmers fleet feet
and the west became re-won –

And under trees, in parks, near peaks,
I can feel your spirit dancing,
and in dark rooms with shaded lamps and faces,
I can feel your spirit singing,
and in buildings, banks and hostiles,
I can feel your spirit weeping,
and in the night, when the moon is bright,
I hear your great big ohm.

Holy Sadness

It's those two rusted red cars,
and that feeling you get when you see them.
sadness
A sadness.
Ah, it's that holy sadness, the sadness that brings with it
the quiet.
Yes.
The sadness that holds the silence,
clasped tight in its little child hands,
ah,
that sadness when the leaves turn
and the morning is cold
and you wear two coats
and you see your breath when you step out the door
and you wished you weren't so poor
and maybe had some mittens.
Yeahp!
That beautiful sadness.
The one your fingers feel,
because they're lacking gloves.
The one you feel
and I mean
feel
because you know

because you know

Maybe

maybe we're all just too caught up in this big sad world
and we can't escape it,
'til there's chickens clucking six feet o'er head
and that big sad world
is our resting bed.

OVER HILLS, OVER HORIZONS

Aquí

al lado de la cama
con dedos en su pelo
ella está sentada –

en la puerta
yo conozco,
el pelo de ella
es una orilla
con bienvenida
para me alma –

aquí
aquí es la paz del mundo

Arnold and Hecht's Woman

Arnold and Hecht
can keep their bitch,
sitting seaside with distraction –
woman wishing to scratch her itch.
She sat with me
an eve or two, we drank and smoked,
tho –
I mirrored her failure Arnold,
staring out to sea,
while she talked at me,
incessantly –
"'stead," I said, "I'm sorry dear,
you may find me queer,
but I'd rather be near
the sea –
so couldn't you just leave me be?"

Afterward,
I sat alone –
comfortably.

whenifeelalive

wheniseeyourbeautyinpictures
thoilay/lieondarkbeds
sofarawayicouldn'tcount
themiles
foramoment
indimlamplight
ifeelthefeeling
inmychest,
theoneifeel
whenyou'renear/
whenifeelalive

Over Hills, Over Horizons

Over hills, overlapping themselves
cool greens caused to waver by cool breeze –
there sits solace, somewhere; solemn faced.

Over horizons, over full stars
upon black-colour space, upon time and existence –
there is immortality;
[– vision of dancing destruction smiling in love...]
....

Man on Church Steps

there is a man walking in rain
with hat pulled down over eyes,
no disguise, just a drizzle
water ripples on the surface
of puddles gathered from the fall –

a woman with shopping cart makes noise
pulling hard wheels over curb
crashing metal grates, they cause a cat
to scatter from the porch of a house
Victorian style ...

looking up at heaven, across the street
on church steps staring out upon the vast horizon
is a different man, he with beard,
his eyes are bright with sun descending
passing behind the mountains

his coat is tattered, beard is dirty,
his pants are matted, mud clings close to bottom hem,
he raises bottle in salute,
brown bag, crumpled smile,
before setting off
toward sunset

Dishes

doing the dishes
is a way of keeping your hands clean –
when my hands are dirty (metaphorically)
I do the dishes
for it is often when my hands are dirty
that there are dishes to be done

That Evening Moment

the hardest part is knowing
you're far across the ocean(s)
and I hardly even know you
anymore
either way

Remember

remember the night I ate the acid
after I walked up to the fellow that
looked like Hunter S. Thompson
and said, "Why, you look like Hunter S. Thompson..."
so he laughed and took me outside
to smoke a cigarette and it turned out
he was Hunter S. Thompson,
some kind of Northern Nevada reincarnation,
some mirror image on the opposite side of the desert...
and we talked as I took drags from my cigarette and he said,
"You like Lucy?"
and I said, "I love Lucy!"
(not talking '50's television here...)
and he took me to the back alley and dropped it on my tongue
before I came in, turning on, talking to cute Korean chicks who
said I looked artistic...

and you laughed and the lot of you talked
while I made eyes at the three of you
before everyone got drunk
and stumbled home in the Reno night...
and you were stumbling arm and arm with Armstrong
and I hung back smiling telling the fellow next to me that
that was real beauty,
that drunk-stumbling, perfect-smiling, Japanese-speaking
chick-in-the-hip-skirt-with-the-shining-eyes...
that that was real beauty,
that chick – drunk stumbling you ...
yeah, that was beauty...

and we stumbled on home and everyone was near passing out,
the boys fell asleep on the couch in a drunken snuggle
they would blush and not admit to in the morning
and I asked if I could lay next to you,
I swore I wouldn't touch,
I knew your boyfriend was in the next city
and I wouldn't do no wrong,
and you smiled while I stumbled over my words,
and you said yes,
and I laid next to you
staring at the ceiling in my stockinged feet,
just talking about everything and nothing,
and I told you – I'm home... I'm a fox who found his burrow... –
and you told me secrets, half-slurred, sleepy words,
before you nodded off

and I sat there in the dark knowing that I would never ....

I remember that time...

A Poor Note (And a Poor Poem)

now, I'm older but not old,
I know it isn't all fireworks and bridges, in front of clock towers,
blooming buds, sweet spring scents,
                (unless of course, when it is)
but I wouldn't mind, for a moment,
       a good year or two of my time
                (or longer if you do not tire of me),
we might make it...

perhaps don't take it sexually,
you see, when I think of making it
it doesn't make me think of sex, sweat,
open windows in cheap motel rooms,
big brand cigarette smoke...
but instead watching you rise from bed,
slowly pulling on your dress
as the sunlight
creeps
through
blinds
tracing
lines
across
your
skin,
of you smiling as you zip the back,
and I pull on my slacks
and we go out and grab a bite before returning,
actually smiling,
even though it has rained so much
these last couple'a
years

Ariadne

on mornings like this,
drinking grainy coffee,
wishing for a cigarette,
I think sometimes
I'll sell all my things,
throw clothes in a bag,
and head over that Atlantic
        to the place from where my grandfather came...

because somewhere there,
        a girl goes lightly...

maybe she would walk with me by flats wearing flats,
looking far from flat in pretty dresses with a pretty smile...

I used to dream, I used to dream a lot... I dreamed last night...

– I feel sometimes I'm creeping around her attic
    I know I probably shouldn't be there
    but I'm being very careful,
    turning pages of small books
    littering the dust covered floor
    with small words in them
    giving me small glimpses
        of a life I've never known...
    sometimes I wish someone
    would walk up to the attic and find me...

I'd stumble, stutter,
trying my best to find some explanation,
some sort of story
to hide the fact that I really meant to be there,
in that exact place, though I knew I shouldn't be...

        because sometimes you can love someone at a glimpse
            without even knowing them ...

Secret

I took the bus,
riding over the 80
as I would do hundreds of times
after that time,
unlike the times to come tho
I didn't sleep,
watched every line
passing under
passing under
passing under ...
I watched the mountains
I remembered from
then, when we were kids
when you kissed all my friends
and never thought to kiss me ...
and after ten or so hours
and after gamblers were dropped off at casinos
I walked through station doors
out to still street
to you standing beautiful,
to you with shining eyes ...
to your house we went
trying to talk all those years
trying to talk them all into thirty minutes ...
we had to sneak in quietly,
your roommate was sleeping,
hated losing sleep,
so we sneaked ...

I said I'd sleep on floor,
you said you wouldn't have it,
we wore pajamas,
I had to borrow some of yours,
we lay still talking
while the television screen flickered
before we kissed
before we ...
... and we stayed in bed til I left a week later ...
I hid tears behind black sunglasses
waving goodbye to you
in casino parking-lot ...

but I don't think you remember it anymore
like a secret you trusted only to me ...

How We'd Make It

hey ariadne, come over sea,
attend a university –
and while you're getting a degree,
make little love with me –

on holiday we'll hit the road,
hitch across America,
with thumbs stretched out and hands to clasp,
we'll count the passing overpass

no newscasters to ruin nights,
just evening under the stars's lights,
in sleeping bags bundled together
we'll make it through the stormy weather

and when you wake I'll kiss your face,
or instead the sun may take my place,
we'll roll our packs, sling em over backs,
then try and thumb for Cadillacs

if at first we don't succeed,
we'll sit on packs sat in the weeds,
we'll roll our smokes and light them up,
and thumb instead for pickup trucks

eventually we'll catch a ride
to take us over asphalt tide,
from where it goes when it dies,
we'll hitch to coast and watch it rise

then back home we'll follow sun,
exhausted, smiling, no need to run,
just sit and stretch out your thumb,
we'll make it like enlightened bums

Song of Sex

every time
a reverse birth, back to a moment before my moment,
moving through the unconscious for one micro-second,
speeding through the vast continuum of each time laid down,
laying lines under star-light, without horn,
only sighs –
sighs escaping like the wind blow,
speeding over mind, deep crevices of brain,
deep crevices pressed to points, pushing through the veil
for instant,
taking another breath.

they said Whitman was barbaric –
perhaps I do not know of barbarism,
only the jissom of man, floating through the vast continuum –
each cunt some doorway speeding the seeing into the next
moment...

my mouth is full of words I dare not speak...

I love each lay as I love myself,
seeing some vast continuum of love, a vortex of unspeakable
sutra,
a closeness most dare not tread...
if I can not hold her, hold her, hold her,
hold her like the first,
like the first time, in half-lit room, with eyes half-open, with
feeling half conscious,
if I can't love her like the first,
like the first face seen,
like the first time looked in mirror,
like the first body that pressed to mine in playground
innocence, sitting under sunrise warming up the sand
holding hands, a sigh escaping lips, curious sound, unfamiliar,
feelings can be unfamiliar though age old, a feeling known
forever, relearned in a moment –

if I cannot remember,
kill me, remember, remember, remember –
the vast continuum of memory laid between legs of lovers,
sweetened snatches made sweeter by the knowledge of the one,
I remember each time, but each time is spread along the conscious,
the vast continuum of each time –
time in San Fran bay area, wine drunk, early morning, holding her before she left,
before we left to bay, instead laid in apartment, half-lit – god was she beautiful –
time in backseat, sitting back behind building in industrial area
time on top of parking garage, beneath the stars, on break from work in middle of the night
time time time
the bodies pressed close, held close,
sweat drips on carpets, couches, dirt and grass,
back of movie theater in darkness, others munching popcorn, pressing into greasy mouths,
muffling sigh, let it not escape to turn their heads from shining screen...

a song of myself, and herself, a song sang silently, the notes only reaching such highs occasionally,
escaping to the world continuum, placing ourselves upon the sound expanse
stretching coast to coast, joining all the songs of lovers laying, here, there, everywhere,
a single song sighed in pleasure, pain – a single song sighing love –
not some love banded together, placed to picture some idea of perfect,
instead a love, that which muffles so much sound it makes itself a secret,
a secret which the whole world knows...

the animals making it... blocked from sight... in bushes... under stars's light...
just like the people making it in apartment beds... above their neighbor's sleeping heads...

some song of sad but beautiful sighed into the sky...

ya, some song of sad but beautiful, sighed into the sky ...

...

Psalms Cigarette

I rolled a cigarette out of Bible paper
        not to be blasphemous but instead just because
        all my books have too thick of pages, save King James'
        tome so thick upon the shelf.

I smoked it out in alleyway
        amongst the scattered ant traps and bottle caps
        and broken glass which litters cement sidewalk.

I really meant no harm or offense,
        I'd use the pages of old Dostoevsky or Kerouac,
        or more fittingly Bukowski,
        if they used the same thin paper which the Psalms so
        often stain.

I only used the page in back,
        the one for reference,
        leaving the scribed words intact
        for different days
        not yet laid
before me.

Sitting Dream in Library

Speak easy, sitting out under the star light
in the library promenade, though the books have long been
blocked, the doors locked hours earlier.
Something to say, it sits on tip of tongue,
we talk and talk, looking here and there and sometimes at each
other, meeting eye gaze for a moment, somehow calming, so
alone in night. I used to have more answers, funny that, for now
I say I know more, don't I, how could I not, got a lot more years
in memory, thinking about that too much sure to be the death
of me. I guess these cigarettes, and another pack after,
somehow sooth the sadness for a minute, though somehow
reminiscent, used to know so much more, and was so certain
sure. I smile sometimes if I think of all the people though,
who smile at me on the street when I smile or say hello,
and somehow sometimes that's the new go –
so sitting here is lovely.

First Full Moon of Winter

I walk with head hung, watching
leaves pass by under feet, the changing colors
gold, orange, red and fading green,
seen crisp and clear through thick winter
air.

Taking deep breaths before an escaping sigh
while all the frosted cars pass by.

Sometimes I see the sun rise over the mountains standing
far far in distance.
It slants through sky and seems to sit in bands that hang
in morning air.
I certainly should see this every day,
but most instead lay in bed
lazily.

Is there kindling for your fire,
for it's certain to need lit.
The summer came and passed
so fast.
No more I see the cats
who so often sat,
perched on
their private
porches.

I wonder where they wandered
to…

Night

the birds have all flown south, their wings cutting
through clouds leading them to warmer places –

warm bodies laid in sand as speckles cling to feather
fabrics –

save for single yellow bird, who wanders bar
with drink in hand and sadly looks my way

oh face familiar, such a sorrow, same eyes illuminated
by dim lamp light, same look as when we last made love

it's been a couple years and as she passes past, our eyes meet
and I remember –

no matter how many drinks I swallow, my stomach
still feels tight, as I light my cigarette, blowing smoke-thought
into

night

SONGS OF SEAS AND CIRCLES

Nostolgic Reproduction

looking over old poems
written by old friends and posted up
on walls forgotten –
messages in words and pictures
faded and misremembered
somehow more beautiful –
it's like Walter Benjamin said,
how there is a certain aura about
the original work
even if
the paint
has faded
as memories
and
emotion
do –

disappearing
in the crowd
of a million faces
each a
painting
each a
past

Variations on Afternoon

I.
I watched a little bird perched
        outside on branch of willow
        through a diamond window
        singing cheery songs in after-
        noon.

II.
A square turned on its side showed
        framed picture of the nature
        viewed from place much different
        than that depicted in the
        shape.

III.
The bird hung before flitting
        darting into great blue
        disappearing in the real air –

        I took a breath and
                stepped outside.

IV.
There was a babe in basket
        draped over with a blanket
        mother pushing it along
        through cold air of after-
        noon.

V.
A cat it crept through alley
        slinking on the sidewalk
        looking over shoulder
        before jumping wire
        fence.

VI.
A girl she walked on, wonderful,
        beautiful as the breeze blow
        I stared as she walked past me
        a smile in the after-
        noon.

These States

I knew a man who drove great distances,
        spanning over miles and miles of highway,
        watching sun rise in the east and set in the west
        all in same day stretch, great trek all across these states.

    He never said a thing about America, he just knew.

So many cars roll over so many stretches of roadways,
        dirt and gravel along the side after cuts created in the
        asphalt, the noise vibrating through the vehicle.

        Semis pass, honking horns to outstretched thumbs of
        hitchers, their skin dark from the sun, slightly tinted
        red from day passed, day ahead still something thought
        about, still a few hours
        before dark.

They hurt on sides of highways,
        leaning on side of parked car, peeing in the cover of the
        wheels smoking cigarettes and staring into distance,
        so much of America stretched out before one that one
        cannot help but weep.

So many small towns stretched over distance, lined up along
>   the mass of white dotted lines which span and act as
>   veins. The veins of this state, through spans of
>   mountains and vast imaginings of flat land
>   making up the middle of these states.

The beauty of these states,
>   the mountains playing purple backdrop to the rising
>   and setting sun, the darkened reflection of the sky,
>   sometimes they blend together
>>   as if in painting.
>   The waterfalls, the ones viewed from the backroads
>>   prove the best, as they make one
>>>   slow their speed
>>>   and stare and stare and stare.

Only Once

Dying is one of the things
that you only get to do once,
that you have some sort of
choice
about...

I thought about eating every flower
I found
walking my way home –
I'm certain one would make me sick,
and perhaps I'd die
throwing up colored petals
on this black asphalt world ...

deflowered...

another thing you get to do
only once ...

Maryland

she's dressed like Maryland ...

blue and white flats with buckle over toes,
stockings strapped to garter belt hidden under skirt,
    pale in color, like the uncovered bit of her legs
        where the stockings end before the skirt begins ...

her cardigan is buttoned high, navy with fine lines –
white to match the skirt – and the blue to match her eyes ...

it is if she came from sea,
    or instead is going ...

like the sun ...

it rose on me in Maryland, the day twenty-some years ago when
    I was born ...

it rose on her some twenty years before she moved out West ...

a thought, a feeling, rising from the infinite water
    lapping at the shores
    of the heart and mind ...

life rising from the infinite water
    lapping on the shores
    of Maryland ...

Breath (A Birthday Poem)

some twenty years ago, your light shined,
      peering through the abyss
            of the pre-exist—
and with open eyes, coughs and cries,
      the world knew something beautiful—
and somewhere, a stranger smiled,
      he hadn't the slightest idea why,
      but it was a silent celebration
                of life—

pressing new existence
        into old existence,
      the world gained a new consciousness
        to join the vast abstract—
heavier and lighter
        all at the very same time—
like every moment of yer life
      leading up into this living moment
                now—

      blow out those candles love—
          your breath is existence,
            new,
              old,
                and otherwise

That Season We Said We Were in Love

remember that season we said
we were in love and you went
all the way across these united states
back to school in cold old chicago town
and we wrote letters back and forth
waking up to new words and old words
lines we writ but did't remember
because too many bottles got swallowed
in the darkness, after the sunset,
and you moved back, came by plane
so we shacked up in a studio
locked in a room trying to strangle
each other, both in and out of bed
(two very different strangles)
and I choked and choked, spitting bile
vile words across wood-floored room,
tears were shed, slammed were the doors—

angry gestures and cold breezes
that blew both inside and out
in the cold season
we said we were in love

If Were Sounds Not People

there are wedding bells ringing everywhere,
and I am a crow sitting on perch of abbey

my horrible voice is cacophonous in comparison
       to such pretty chimes

she looks beautiful in that wedding dress,
walking through the flowered garden,
a fountain falling gentle water, petals
floating on the calm reflecting surface

(for such beautiful ceremony the cloud
       cover sure seems heavy ...)

'caw' 'caw' says the crow,

'chime' 'chime' says the bell,

and somewhere in the distance,

the sound of a child crying ...

Your Breath (A Little Bird Told Me)

I buried a tiny bird today, in the rocky patch
out back, just beyond the gate,
where weeds grow near the garden and
the shade of a young tree hangs
over the sunken hole

and as I buried that little bird,
who was black with white belly
who had white spots, pokadots,
trailing up black back and feathered
wings, I watched the wind gently
move those ruffled feathers,
ever so slightly, like flight without
movement

it is funny, for I thought this is
how your breath must be, cigarette and
coffee smell, as you blow smoke out
with a smile, fragile, like porcelain,
so easily broken, like the little body
now buried in the backyard

but still something else, like a final
flight, after the sun light has disappeared,
when all the birds are nested,
save for solely one, still feeling the
breeze beneath outstretched wings,

alone, beatific,
soaring on the back of soft breath
escaping from your lips

Entirely

I want you entirely ...

sprawled out, half wrapped in sheets as hair sticks up reaching toward the sun
like yellow flowers

entirely,

cursing, spitting, scowling, with horrible words falling out your throat past
red-stained, wine-rouged lips

entirely,

sitting in the mud with dirty knees and arms wrapped around sad horses for the slaughter –
the unbearable lightness of being

entirely,

weeping with something beautiful, the rippled clouds rolling over, mixing shadows
and the sun

entirely,

as the world turns, ticking hours away from time clock, and we grow older and sadder
and ever-so more grey

entirely,

with crows in both our arms, and black birds tangled in your hair, walking with two rolls,
smiling, as there buzzes past a bee

entirely,

every bad poem you've ever jotted, balled up in little fist and thrown away –
I would dig up the remains just to save them from decay

entirely,

while you're dancing, kicking feet, smiling, flailing, laughing, with ears ringing
from the blues player

entirely,

so much so I'd swim across the sea ...

Love

all I want to do
is be enveloped by you

so I can be poetry,

and not simply
write it

Spring Showers

sittin' in
the rain, sittin' in
a puddle, just sittin' there
next to the pool reflectin'

holdin' hands and sittin' there
by that pool and talkin', smilin',
wonderin' what they're doin' in that temple,
we can see their shadows, the silhouettes in windows
and the rain, the rain it falls

seems some sort of ritual,
and we watch, soaked in rainfall,
next to that pool reflectin'
the image of their temple
lit up by the lamp light,
even now near midnight,
far past the time they recommend
the people to be out

we take another pull from flask
and laugh and laugh and laugh

the flowers are starting to blossom,
ah, the washing rain
of spring

Just Dreaming Again

I drink wine in the afternoon and stare out across the city
spanning just outside my window, climbing up the mountains

I think, the sun, where it sits, sat in the same place
seven hours ago for you, and he has already went to sleep
as you lay your head to rest in darkness

I wonder, if after I get a fancy education, and get my thoughts
and mind and heart in order, if I could come across the pond
and place a band upon your finger

I'll be a bird perched on your shoulder
        I'll be your love and we'll grow older

and you can show me all the things I've never seen

Jazz Fragment (Bird)

bird perched on telephone wire backdropped in blue
      white, white feathers, so unspeckled, shining in the
      sun

    like the porcelain bird,
          sitting 'cross the sea,
          the one that sits on window sill
              in await of me …

Touch

you make the world seem so much bigger and
        so much smaller all at the very same time,

as if I am young again and I can see across the entire
        horizon, and even past such, to where the sun goes, to
            where the sun continues, forever and forever,
                as if I'm staring into the
                    infinite

you make the world seem so familiar,
        as if nothing could ever invoke a fear, because
            I know now there is a beauty, there is a light,
                there is that thing that some explain
                    as God

you make the stars seem close enough to touch,
        and I wonder if it would be exactly that,
            my fingertips upon your frame ...

Poem Bridge

I'm building a bridge
from every poem I've ever written,
it's motley colored and quite rag-tag
and I wouldn't step on every surface,
for some of the strophes are shoddy and
wont hold much weight

I figure one for every mile,
so I got a lot more to write,
sitting up late night
second pot of coffee
jotting and jotting,
sticking each page
up into the sky

one day I'll walk across,
disappearing in the stars
you hold behind your tongue
and in your tiny hands,
smelling of ink and
cigarettes

Train Dream

last night I had a dream
that we were riding on a train
and as it sped along the wind
rushed through the cabin
tussling your hair and making you
wrap your arms around your frame

I was wearing a big old jacket,
wine stained and torn, but thick
like the kind you see on
railroad men in winter —
I took it off and wrapped you
in it

you pulled the coat over your bare arms
and we huddled in a corner close
to each other, and you smiled at me
and I could feel your breath on my face
between gusts of wind,
and I could tell because it was warm
and I awoke expecting condensation
on my cheek

and we laughed lightly to ourselves,
and you snuck a little closer to me,
but I was shy and my hands rested
on my knees and my stomach turned
nervously

you leaned your head on my shoulder
and as soon as I felt that weight
I was alone again,
laying in an empty room

Heavy Love

love
is a heavy thing
when compared to
the unbearable lightness
of being

so I might need a little help
in lifting it
up into the sky

if you'll help,
we'll gather threads
and tether them to birds

we'll run like kids with kites,
carrying that love upon our backs
'til the wind picks up

until it drifts up

to the sky

Gone

"Justin's fuckin' gone man,
he went off, disappeared down south,
and I don't think he's coming back,
it's sinister"

we sit and smoke cigarettes
watching the sunrise,
and Mike blows smoke out his mouth,
spits on the sidewalk

"Justin's fuckin' gone man,
he went off to find god,
and he ain't coming back –

his preacher hooked him
up to blood machines,
and they've got him
sitting in a shrink's office

it's all shit,
fucking shit"

he spits again

"it's all shit
fed from the asshole
of god"

Heavy Love II

just
lay down

lay
lay
down

just lay down,
put soft hands
on the space
where legs
meet hips

pulling
closer
hips
on
hips
on hips

pulling closer

sigh,

pulling closer,

sigh –

that
heavy
love ...

Could You Just Tell Her?

I knocked on the door, knowing full well
        she wasn't home and wasn't going to answer,
                instead her mother stood in the passageway
                      looking at me suspiciously,

I said,
        "I know your daughter isn't home, but I wonder
        "if you could tell her something for me,
        "just a few words I never said, never got to say:

"tell her that I never got the chance to tell her,
        "but I always felt like I could love her, if she'd let me
"tell her, though we might have been lost in black smoke,
        "with our eyes glazed lazing beneath floorboards,
                "minds hidden in haze
"I was always the highest because I was laying next
        "to her there,
                            lost –

        "and I know you hate me,
        "and even if she were here you probably wouldn't let
        "me speak to her, but I want you too to know,
        "I could have loved her
        "if she'd have let me,

        "could you just tell her that? ..."

her mother stared at me, silently,
        I turned and walked down the dimly lit hall,
        bulb burning, flickering, fighting the sun
        as I opened the door ...

Jazz Chorus I

Oh,
I am a simple charlatan,
        prob'bly not kiddin'
pennin' bits of poesy
        long late into the lamplight —

the here and now,
        I'm figurin' out
is something so
        eternal

so difficult to not
        disappear eternities away
in frames
        of doubt

don't pout,
        my darling dear,
there is no fear
        with you here near,

              ya hear?

The High and the Low Notes

I sit in the dark
when the block is silent
and sing songs to you
as the street lamp light
peeks through blinds
painting lines on white
walls and picture frames,

you're a thousand miles
away so I doubt you
hear the notes, which
is well for I lack melody
and the melancholy
makes my voice crack
even in this whispering
falsetto

Song of Sea and Circle

I dreamt of you again last night,
funny that
whenever I dream of you, we never do
much,
always found sitting somewhere,
bodies tucked real close,
like we're real cold,
though I've never felt
so warm.

They say before the Fall
humans found themselves entwined
two together,
a complete circle.
But after, we were split in two,
souls to circle
in attempt
to find their other half.

When I have these dreams
and when I wake,
I feel a circle.
If only for a moment.

You know,
I was born on the East Coast,
and if it weren't for that Atlantic,
our villages would have neighbored.

I think sometimes souls get scattered
over spans of surly seas...

seas I'd cert'nly swim to be,
the circle that is you and me.

A Poem Concerning Jeff Who Died

So Jeff,
I heard you died.

I used to call you 'old man,'
because you were always calling me
by name of 'boy.'

You smoked Pall Mall
filterless,
sitting in the corner of coffee shop,

and drank your coffee black,
laughing at all the young kids
under your smoky breath.

I heard you died.
I had a feeling last time I saw you,
briefly,

you were looking sickly,
still puffing cigarettes, eyes
scanning thick books.

I wonder sometimes when I walk away,
if this may be the last time I see a person,
turns out last time, the wonder was warranted ...

Univeristy Haiku

Going to university
to get my
misanthropy degree

Dionysus Mourning

"Oh Ariadne," said Dionysus,
standing at the side of seaway,
staring up at Helios
to only see the face
of the goliath's grand-daughter.

The water was calm that day,
but the whole sky stood cloud covered,
parting only to frame the titan's
solar semblance.

"Your grand-daughter has hurt me greatly,
titan," said Dionysus staring at the sun.

Helios stood silent in reply.

EPILOGUE

Song of the Corona Borealis

I. : A Call to 9 Muses

This tale was told a long time ago, but it has been some time
since it has been reworded—though played throughout
so many histories it has found itself,
time and time again.

To tell it I must muster all I have,
I hope my hearing is keen, so my ears may
fall on the voices of muses, and my mind
will be carried by their swaying current,
lacing melodies of beauty flowing out
unto the sea of seas,
                      the blue space so far above …

What I am saying is …

                Let the muses gather 'round, let their voices
reverberate these walls—

Oh Euterpe, let your melody sing eulogies,
so that those life-times past are fresh
in recollection and sorrowful memories
may be sung.

Oh Melpomene sing with your sister
Thalia, so that two sides of the mask are
known, and we may smile and weep
with the words which issue forth.

And Oh! Erato, of course, for that is what
these lyrics be—love—the song of which
you sing, as the snow it blankets the world
in white.

And Calliope and Clio, for that is what
these verses ring—the epic history
enlaced in dream …

To Aoide, of the eldest three,
> so I may find the voice to sing ...

And she of blood anew,
birthed not so long ago—
> Coronet—the muse of clicking keys,
>> for she aids in finding each letter the poet needs.

And finally,
> she of whom these verses be ...

It begins ...

> let these voices
> aid these songs ...

II. : Of Ariadne and Dionysus

Oh Ariadne, she of labyrinths, the dark passages
> not unlike our souls, where rats scurry across
> floors, unseen, and pass over bare feet.

She who knows the monster, for it is she who keeps
> it, and it is she who keeps one from its wrath,
>> though forever devour, it is bound to do ...

>> To rest in chest, swallowing the sorrowful, who abandon
>>> all hope before they adjust their eyes to darkness ...

She who holds the tether, allowing the mad to venture
> into the passages within/without, and if careful—
> holding to her hope she holds in eyes—to venture
> out again, even after meeting with the minotaur.

Yes Ariadne, the petulant orchid, laid soft on river water,
> floating down the current of time, changing
> water into wine, flighty in response to intensity,
> as he burns on river banks, unallowed in water.

Yes he, re-birthed with seasons, bearded and in solace
    when the snow appears and the world becomes
    a virgin white.

He, who in the spring, when buds begin to bloom,
    and the world she blossoms like a blushing maid,
    becomes fresh faced and youthful, smiling in his seduction
    as he disappears with her, laughing, in blankets of green
    and flower fabrics.

Dionysus, dancing, drunk with moment, as the world
    gets hot and fuller, leaves blossoming her figure
    into woman-hood, and summer is found, then fall—
    as she becomes beautiful, heavy with harvest.

He who watches his floating flower,
    as he sits on shore so far away ...

III. : Before the Ship with Black Sails

On the shores of Naxos is where some say he first found her,
    but it was long before this that caught his eye.
    Oh yes, you see, for years he watched her weave, for this
    was one of her many gifts, to tether threads together
    in tapestry which told all tales of time.
    And while she wove, she often sang, quiet songs just unto
    herself about the many sights that she had seen, and the
    many times her heart had hurt as her pale body shook,
    and the moonlight fell in through the windows
        and she cried.

In fact, it was her song which he of mortal mother first took notice,
    for the melody, enchanting, awakened memories, of the womb
    of Semele, and his birthplace near the sea.

    So he sat out, under window, dressed as fox, unseen like
    dream, and listened to her sing,
    until the light of morning,
    for so many mornings.

And in the afternoons when he would wake
> from long sleep and dreams
> of her tunes beneath the moon, he would sing her songs
> she'd never hear, playing his horn out unto the sea.

> For so many months he played, and sometimes he thought
> she knew somehow, and sometimes she'd look out of her
> window, out into the night, and stare out into the darkness —
> sometimes he could swear her stare was exactly pointed
> > where he stood ...

Sometime around these times was when the wind, she shifted, and a
> different breeze blew off the sea. Twas around then the
> strange ship appeared in port —
> > a ship decorated with sails
> > > the color of the aether
> > > which surrounds the stars.

IV. : Of Theseus and Ariadne

Who could blame her — the boy was beautiful —
> he stepped off of his ship and heads turned,
> gazes fixed on his curls, loose, framing his
> well-structured face.

> He shined with the strength of the warriors from his region,
> > and when the people looked upon him
> > a breath of change was said to overtake them.

His breath befell sweet Ariadne as he spoke unto the court
> and claimed that he was a soul for sacrifice, or a
> soul to slay the beast —

> he said that he would save all those to come, but
> first he would save himself — and Ariadne heard this,
> and so she swore that she would save the savior,
> and so start the cycle of salvation.

With the coming of the fellow, who went by name of Theseus,
> there was much celebration, and late did the people
> party, drinking wine and cheering for the possibility
> of change which floated on the air.

And Dionysus floated through the crowd, his breath
moving from mouth to mouth—the wine
painted each person's lips, and all the songs were sung,
and all praises were pronounced.

And when the night grew late, and the sounds settled
    but did not die, Ariadne sought the stranger Theseus,
    and smiled her best smile as she spoke to him
    soft words.

    She said, "Here, take this spool of string, tis of the finest
        I have woven and so certain it is to not break.
        Leave it as your path, like a light which will guide
            you.
        After your victory come back—
        Each person already sings songs of you in their
        head, drunken with the hope you've spread."

He knew the look in her eyes, and after offering a smile,
    took the string and disappeared in the shadows
    of the dying streets ...

V. : The Labyrinth and the Minotaur

The caverns of the labyrinth are a dark place that few men
    dare wander, for there are many things to see within
    the darkness so deep that not a shade of grey is seen.

Few men find the fire, can adjust their eyes to seeing without
    seeing, traversing deeper, both physically as well as
    mentally, to recesses rarely reached.

Even Dionysus, who had been around, watching, playing
    songs upon his horn, only knew so deep into the labyrinth,
    and only dared to wander far under cover of the fox's
    skin, which let him move past the monster—though
    there had been times the beast had certainly sensed the
    wandering venturer ...

        He had certainly seen the steppenwolf within
            that maze, if not the minotaur itself ...

Yes, so it was into the labyrinth the young hero Theseus went,
    and the people stared upon him with high their hopes,
    and Ariadne smiled at him brightly as he stepped into
    the darkness of the maze ...

Ah! The sheer size! The hero imagined how monstrous that inside
    must be—for the closer he came, the more he was certain
    he wasn't imagining—below his feet the floor did rumble
    with the inhale and exhale of the great fear deep within.

It was then he came upon it—without warning it lunged out from the
    darkness, a surprise of sheer force, forcing the hero through
    the air to come to crash upon the wall far across the
    room.

    Twas like a hulking shadow, and before again was seen,
    before his head stopped reeling, the beast had disappeared
    back into the darkness.

    The hero drew his sword and eyed the torch laying
    on the ground across the room, dimly lighting the string
    seen trailing the path back.

    Twas this sight that urged him
    forward, and as the metallic shine of his sword refracting
    the dim torchlight shimmered his place in room, the beast
    began a second charge ...

    Theseus too, charged forward, and as he readied his sword,
    all his focus on his foe, the fellow fumbled over the string—
    this forward lunging, with the way the fellow's luck be,
    caused the sword to slide straight through the creature's
                                             throat.

    It came to crash atop its conquerer,
        and Theseus struggled to catch his breath,
        while sliding the massive body from his chest ...

VI. : Of Proposed Matrimony

There was no doubt that she had saved him, and he pondered this as he followed her string back through darkened passageways, as rats scurried 'round his feet and he stumbled tripping over rubble littering the corridors.

And so when he emerged and all the people stood wide-eyed, with new hopes held within their optics, he smiled at the one called Ariadne, and when the sounds had settled down, he asked her to sail the sea with him and return to his own lands, where she would be his bride.

> And in the joyous crowd, Dionysus watched
> as all the people's hopes floated up into the sky—
>
> as his was preparing to sail herself across the sea,
> a bride to be ...

VII. : Olympus and Athena

It had been some time since Dionysus had visited the mount
  they call Olympus, where some of his kin, some
  not so fond of him, resided.

When he arrived he walked past Hephaestus, sitting looking haggard,
  offering an uninterested smile at the youngest of the gods—

He also passed the glare of Hera, her hatred apparent in her fiery
  gaze—the god of wine just another of the many reminders
  of her Zeus' other lays ...

He paid the old hag little mind as he continued stride,
  wondering where Athena was, for twas her he
  sought, for many reasons ...

> You see, for now that Theseus was a hero,
> he held a halo, granted to him by the patroness of those
> who wander out and conquer that they seek within the
> world—he had made himself of Athena's brood, and

Dionysus hated to imagine her wrath if he simply
slayed his rival ...

    Further, Athena was a cunning lady, who often
had solutions to that which seemed insolvable, and
certainly Dionysus could use such wisdom in the sad
position he now found himself sitting inside ...

He found her first upon the wind, as if the breeze had just
    blown past the leaves of an olive tree—the scent
    carried past his nose.

    Her eyes gleamed and he moved uncomfortably
        when her gaze first fell upon his person—
        her intensity was of such strength it dwarfed
        even his own.

    "Oh my kin," he started, nearly stuttering,
        "I seek your aid, for you see the Fates have
            played a dirty trick on your's truly ...
    "Clotho started spinning the tale, and weaved
        it within my heart in the form of a spinner,
        sitting, singing, far below the stars ...
    "Then Lachesis drew her sticks and set to motion
        the movement which we now sit within,
        bringing forth black sails on the horizon ...
    "But Oh! My dearest kin—my sister on the mountain—
        please do not let Atropos cut the chord,
        the one now inwoven, deep within ... !"

Athena stood expressionless, and her eyes trailed to
    the Glaucus, the owl staring in conversation
    only she could understand.

    The goddess spoke no words in response, but instead allowed
    one corner of her lips to curl in a small smile
    offered to her youngest kin.

    He knew that she would not agree to bring harm to those
    she acted harbinger to, but still her smile told him
    that she would speak unto the fates—and in her eyes,
    shining with their wisdom, too he knew, her plans
    for the fellow with the sails of black ...

VIII. : Of Athena and Theseus

Now this is where we come to Naxos, the place in which
    many have begun this tale being told, and so here
    one may find things familiar, but also things
    unspoken of, since telling and remembering are
    two very different trades ...

    Many days were spent on that island, and the two,
    now together, shared the sun on afternoons as the
    waters rushed along the beaches and brushed the
    sparkling sand.

    Ariadne stared at Theseus as his body shined, wet
    with beads of water as he surfaced from his swims,
    his curls intact even with water rolling from thier tips,

    and it was beautiful.

Dionysus watched, a bum on the beach,
    wandering through the cities with his eyes half open,
    waiting with uncertainness and shallow breath.

    At night he sat out near the sea and relaxed, letting his
    horn sing, the sound ringing out over the waves to
    disappear and fall unheard within the span of water.

    Sometimes he wondered if the sound it traveled,
    somehow traversing 'cross the building-tops and
    finding way inside her window, weaving
    songs which found their form in dreams,
    as she rested peacefully.

Dionysus never asked Athena what she said to Theseus,
    and doubted she would have ever answered anyway,
    for her ways were of an understanding laced with wisdom
    un-understandable by most regardless.

    But late into the night, when the moon was high —
    Phoebe and Selene, the sisters of one body and
    two faces, the light and dark sides of the moon

—were staring over the earth's face full,
Athena came upon the resting Theseus.

      Her voice carried through the room in
words only the hero could hear ...

      When he turned his gaze toward the source,
instead of finding the goddess, he found the Glaucus—
            the eyes of the creature intense and wise.

      Upon him was bestowed a vision of his return
to Athens ...

          The vision made his eyes blur, and tears welled
          within him, overbrimming from his optics and
          rolling down his cheeks—black sails and suicide,
             sorrow ... but hope ...

          There was a great field before him, there was a path
          in the depths of hell, his physical feet stepping
          through the ethereal, the aether of the neverworld ...
             but ...

      Hope ...
As all the people back in Minos had sang of ...

IX. The Departure of the Black Sails

An empty bed and empty beach, beautiful, was what she woke to.
      She looked out across the water, smiling, wondering where
          her lover went, thinking he had wandered to another
          room.

      She wrapped herself in sheet and walked through
          passageways, the sun cast on her skin made it glow,
          and it matched her face until her smile
             began to fade ...

      Where was he?

After pulling on her dress she wandered out and walked
along the beach. Not a soul stood out there, and
when she placed her hand over her eyes to stare out
towards the port she could not see his ship
resting in the docks ...

She knew immediately,
and stared out across the sea, as the waves rolled in,
indifferently.

Dionysus too, walked along the beach, and while he walked he
pondered —
he had watched the ship leave port early in the morning,
and so he wandered through the city in a haze dull
and curious. He felt a bit ethereal, a ghost, for though
the other had left the isle, he pondered if he had
done the right — it was a strange feeling, he thought,
this moral quandary ...

So to the wine he went.
And by the time the moon found her place above the
sky, his lips had found themselves well stained with
a shade of rouge.

This was when he saw her
with her sad eyes, sitting behind the bar,
staring out across the ocean as a warm
breeze blew in from out above the blue.

Drunk and brave, he took up his horn, and after
telling the band to loosen up and get a little
jazzy, Dionysus started in on the tune of
'It's Only a Paper Moon.'

She smiled as he sung out, and behind him it was
curious, for a group of gulls landed on the
beach behind the band, and
because it was so dark of night,
they looked like silhouettes outlined by moonlight,
standing afront the backdrop
of the rolling sea.

X. : Dionysus' Idea

> So this was how it went for many weeks,
> > the moon she saw more than a few full cycles,
> > with Dionysus drinking, singing, lighting up
> > the eyes of Ariadne beneath the spans of the black
> > above.

And every evening after she departed Ariadne walked alone,
> her feet in sand on beach, faint footprints Dionysus
> would later find as he made his way on home.

> > No matter how many songs he sang, she never spoke to him,
> > > but some nights when he played sad songs
> > > quiet tears would trail down her gentle face
> > > and she would raise to lips her drink.

> > So he would wander around the city streets, long after
> > > everyone was asleep, and when he followed those
> > > faint footprints in the sand disappearing in the
> > > lapping water, it was simply so it seemed he had
> > > a place to go after all the bars had closed.

> > There was a sadness that permeated the deity's own mind,
> > > even heavier than hers, whom he held so high—
> > > for it was not entirely Theseus who had brought
> > > her tears—but twas Dionysus' doing more than any…

> > He stayed up late, watching the slow crawl of the stars,
> > > staring out across the waters that lapped on shores
> > > of Naxos. He gazed above, and it was then an idea
> > > blossomed in his mind—for the time it now was
> > > spring, and the doings in this tale had seen the cycle
> > > of the seasons …

> > > He would place in the stars her crown, and it would
> > > > be his gift,
> > a band forever shining in the sky, a keepsake through the
> > centuries, to hang above and smile down upon her head.

He would weave her throughout history, a myth and beautiful saintress — a muse to light the dark paths of the labyrinth, a patron of those who wander through dark corridors to overcome those things which lay within to find those gifts bestowed upon the devout and the adventurous upon their
    travel's end.

        Perhaps then would she smile again …

XI. : Hermes' Gift

This time he of the grapes needed not venture all the way to Olympus
    to seek his kin — for Hermes wandered all around the country-
        sides and could be found by those who knew how to go about
            that they sought —

        You see, the secret is to wait 'til dusk, when the lights
            are getting low all across horizon.
            It is then you can hear his horn —
            the sweet jazz of the message-
            bearer bearing his message to the
            changing sky, fading to oranges and
            reds, then purples,
            then the black.

And that is how he found him, and smiling
    Dionysus bared his horn and blew with his cool brethren —
    Hermes' sound more smooth than the brash blows of his
                             pupil.

    The two played into the night, and when they finally grew
        tired, they laughed and talked over a fire, burning in
        the middle of a green, green field — dark but lit by the
        single-bodied sisters —

It was then Dionysus asked his brother to craft for him a pen —
    A pen gifted with poetry which would write words so strong
        that once laid down they'd cast stars up to the sky, so
        beautiful they'd make criers cease to cry and those
        with somber faces to find tears within their eyes.

>Words that would fly up into the great blue, like
>> blackbirds,
> that once they reached past atmospheres would
>> alight into
> the most intoxicating of constellations
>> that would forever be
>>> a silent song singing her name ...

>> Ariadne.

To these words Hermes had a hardy laugh,
> but because he loved his brother he agreed upon his wishes,
> though he warned the other to be careful of his meddling,
> for dangerous it can be, for one to play with those three,
>> the Fates ...

So the gift was given, and after a night of wine drinking,
> the brothers parted ways, promising to again jam someday,
> though Hermes' joked if that would be fate, or if Dionysus
> would instead find some sort of horrific karmic debt —
> perhaps in form of death ...

XII. : Psalacantha

> Hermes always had a certain sense of humor that
> could at times come across as unsettling — and this was
> something Dionysus knew — but he could not quite shake said
> feeling as he walked along on home ...

> So, to alleviate his mind and slow himself for
> sleep, he stopped at one of the bars on a side street on his way
> through city. There were a good amount of people sitting in
> the thin light, and Dionysus was served in short time — he
> stared out at the sea thinking of his situation and the sadness
>> he had caused ...

>> But the poetry within his pen would alleviate his sin,
>> or so he liked to imagine ...

It was then he was interrupted from his wanderings in feeling —
> a woman spoke and smiled as she stared at his sad facade,
> she said,
>> "You're looking full of sorrow, and tired I would say,
>>> a lady, likely, that's what I'd imagine, I'll tell
>>> you, if that is the case, you must not lose
>>>> your hope —
>>> but in the meantime, you mustn't lose your
>>> touch, so you might as well walk home with
>>> me, and I will help you 'til the time
>>>> you find her for forever —
>>> or whatever exactly it is you've got imagined,
>>> up inside that imaginin' head …"

She said her name was Psalacantha,
> and plants hung all about her top floor apartment, which contained within
>> a window facing west, which allowed the sun to shine in
>>> during
>>>> evening times.

>> She undressed in the living room, nonchalantly, and as her dress fell
>> to the floor she stared up him with eyes narrowed …

>> She walked carefully, her bare-feet barely
> leaving ground as she glided closer to the slightly drunken
>> Dionysus —

but when she came real close, he rose, and said he had to go …

>> She said it was too late to leave, that the two were
>>> meant for company,
>> and that she had no problem if still he sought his other lady,
>>>> if only
>>> he would stay, and be with her as well,
>>>> tucked there within the leaves …

Again he tried to leave, but again this was something she would
> not allow — instead a smoke billowed from her pores, and
> seemed too to pour from the leaves of those surrounding
>> plants.
> The walls all folded upon his person and suddenly the span
> of time

And it was here Dionysus became lost for several years …

So many days lost in the haze — the sun once came through window
        and a whisper wafted past the ear of the dazed
        Dionysus, paralyzed with memories
            unremembered in his head —

        It was then he remembered his Ariadne, and her face acted
            as the
                sun on the haziest of days
                    bursting through the blue to
                shine light on all the grey surrounds of all
                those wandering around.

Recalling that his pen rested just within his pocket, Dionysus then
        began to pen a poem, his words weaving within each other,
            lacing together
            to place a story upon the page —
                and as he wrote his captor began to fade,
becoming one   with
                the surrounding greenery, just
another plant   in the foreboding
              scenery
                  of the cell she called
apartment.

        He was free — so he rushed outside,
            out into the sunshine shining on
            his tired smile...

                and he hurried off into the distance.

XIII. : Hell

He came upon the city near the time of dusk,
        and all the people of Naxos were out wandering,
        some along the shore, and many more in the streets —
            it was strange, for it was rare for so many people
            to be out and about at once, for different folks
            were usually out at certain times throughout the
            day …

Making way through the people standing—or too shuffling,
    trying to make their own way through the crowd—
    Dionysus soon came toward the city's outskirts,
    where the crowd grew thicker and
    to which the current of movers seemed to be
    moving toward …

And it was there he found his horror,
    hanged up in branches of a willow tree—
                  Ariadne.

They said it was all too much, the people whom she spoke to on
    occasion—they said that Theseus' abandonment,
    followed by the disappearance of the drunken
    horn player, caused her heart a sickness she could not
    drown in drink.

    Her little body could not bare the rolling waves of the
    seas of sorrow, constantly exaggerated by the sound of
    the water lapping at the shores each and every evening …

        And the worst thing—
           it was all Dionysus' doing …

He ran away from the scene, down to the sandy beach,
    the same place he had followed her footprints,
    faint, light and little, oh so long ago—
        no footprints now, only sandy ripples,
    repainted each time the waves rolled in.

He wept. How he wept—running out into the water,
    screaming, near-drowning as the waves crashed
    against his person and he lost his footing, so being
    swept into the sea.

His curses echoed through the indifferent night, and
    upon his breath foul cries came upon the name
    of Hades and his horrid bride Persephone—
    whom he was certain had some doing in this
    due to her forever loathing of things beautiful
    throughout the year, for it is her fate to be in the
    inferno during certain seasons …

Well, his words did not disappear into the wind or sea you
see, and Hades' ears heard the curses upon his
bride —
With whispers to his brother, god
of seas,
Hades had Dionysus swallowed by
the tide, pulling
his person to the depths
to personally apologize
to Persephone ...

When Dionysus awoke he found himself face to face with the god
of death himself, he some know as Hades — the one and only.
The older of the brothers cleared his throat and raised his
brow before his sullen voice spoke out,

"Tisk, tisk — twas you then little brother —
if I should even call you such a
thing, some bastard if I
remember quite
correctly — am I right?"

Hades paused a moment, though not long enough
to allow for answer,

"Well then, will you apologize? Or shall I
take your eyes? Or mouth? Or
maybe just your tongue, so
you mayn't talk your way
from out of so many
situations, and into so
many others ... ?

"Or maybe I will simply keep you here, and
end your senseless cycle, old age
and youth, and back
around again ... ?"

Dionysus cleared his throat, standing solidly upon his feet,

"Instead, how 'bout we cut a deal? I apologize and you
allow me to retrieve a soul from beyond the Styx
and bring her back
my bride-to-be?"

Hades laughed,

> "How about if you can retrieve your
> bride-to-be from the same
> situation in which she
> aided he? But for you,
> no string, only the talent
> you
> yourself do
> bring …"

Immediately Dionysus found himself at mouth of labyrinth,
the yawning darkness awaiting the silent swallowing
of his still-wet figure …

XIV. : The Labyrinth and the Doppelganger

And so he strode into the entrance, the darkness so intense
it swallowed him seemingly before he even came
upon it, for all sight disappeared with only a few
small strides forward.

A feeling of foreboding swallowed Dionysus as quickly as
the darkness, and the hair upon his arms and neck
arose as if a chill had traveled to his very bones.

He took a deep breath and continued forward …

> Skeletons seemed to dance within the darkness,
> though he could see absolutely nothing as
> he walked along, running his fingers
> upon the wall to understand the curving
> and contorting caverns—
> > he could sense them, as if their
> > fingers trailed just a
> pace behind him, and he was certain if they
> ever touched him he would perish—wither
> like the plants in winter …

    Death seemed all about
        as he wandered along—breathing deep he
        allowed his mind to wander to the brighter
        things, the look he knew so long ago, her
          lips lightly curled in faint smile ...

    Death seemed all about
        and as he wandered along, feeling through
        the dark, his mind lost focus and guilt
        and sorrow came over him like the waves at
        highest tide. He thought of the words
        of Hermes when the two had parted in what
        seemed so long ago—of his karmic debt
        and possible death—that inevitable
        possibility held for each and every person
        upon any certain day ...

Hermes ...

    It was that name which brought the light in darkness,
       and deeper in the labyrinth, he could see the light
       of fire. And just then his hand fell to his pocket,
       coming to rest upon his pen ...

        Bringing the point of the seed of poetry to
       a crumpled piece of parchment, the one overcome
       with sorrow began to write a poem ...

And it was then the beast stepped forth from darkness,
         and Dionysus looked upon his face.

        Yes—his face—Dionysus' own—
          another he, staring back at he,
           smiling ...

The doppelganger stared at his double,
    and Dionysus could hardly believe his eyes.

    The other spoke with tones exactly like his own,
       and the sound of its voice was quite unsettling
       in its familiarity,

"Oh, are you so surprised?"
            it said, a smirk upon its face,

"Did you truly expect a beast? A physical
            challenge for you to overcome? Ha!
            Come now! You must have known
            what you would find within this
            maze before you even
            stepped inside ...

"You are the greatest beast that could
            possibly be, yes, you, not even me —
            the most horrid of atrocities —
            tis in this maze a monster like
            yourself should forever be ..."

The words brought Dionysus to his knees,
        and he kneeled in darkness as tears stained lines upon his
        dirty face.

    He wept and wept, and over the sounds of his sobs the
            horrible creature who was he berated him, saying the
            foulest things, all true of his actual deeds ...

    He wept and wept, reaching his hands up to his face to wipe
            away the tears which flooded his eyes and then rolled
            over the rest of his features ...

He wept until the dirt which covered his
            filthy hands had all disappeared,
        and when he rose his head, after his final tears were shed,
        he realized that he was only one, sitting in the
            center
                of the labyrinth.

            And,
                    Ariadne slept comfortably on a bed in corner,

                        in the slowly shifting light of fire,

                            beautiful.

XV. : Dionysus Departs Hades

    Though the time was joyous due to the reclamation of the one
        he loved, Dionysus still found his head hung heavy
        as he traversed the path which would lead him from
        the maze. Ariadne slept within his arms as he walked,
        and when he stared down at her face he could not
        help but feel great pangs of sorrow — for was it he
        with whom she even wished to be — and after so
        much time was the answer to said question even
        relevant — or had the sea of sorrow washed away any
        hope of a pleasant reality at the end of this sad
                adventure ... ?

Dionysus pondered all these things as he walked along his way, and
    as he emerged from the gaping maw at the head of labyrinth
    Hades greeted him with the most curiously horrid of smiles,
        and his eyes shined wickedly as he asked,
                "Did you find what it was you
                        sought
                        within?"

Dionysus stood silently staring at his brother,
    his lips pressed together tightly.

        After silence passed a moment
        the solemn-faced god
        spoke in stolid tones,
            "I have done the task you asked of me,
                accept it as my apology,
                now I ask you to allow my leave ..."

    Hades smirked, clearly pleased with the look
        deep within the gaze of Dionysus, the gaze of one
        who has looked at death and felt the pain of
        time to pass, time passing, and the times past ...

                "Very well, my little
                      bastard brother,
                      you may find your
                      path back to surface —
            do say hello to the sun for me ..."

    And so Hades departed,
                still smiling ...

XVI. Dealings with Aion and Chronos

When reaching surface, Dionysus placed the still-sleeping Ariadne
        in a comfortable bed in a fine room, and then
        went walking out into the city streets,
        thinking of how he had made a mess of things.

He thought of when he first had seen her — when she was still smiling,
        bright like the sun and a gift to be seen when walking through
        the streets, spreading her blessing through the world ...

Yes, she was beautiful before he had ever interfered — even in her love
        for another — for in her love she was beautiful, and so her love
        was beautiful, even if it was no love of his ...

    He began to hatch a plan, and the thought of things hatching
        found him traveling to the edge of atmosphere, just
        out there near the end of world egg.

    It was here, so far above the clouds, he found the floating isle,
        where the fountain so often spoke about in myths,
        the one which renews all things which drink from it,
                flows from a source
                unknown ...

Here by this fountain he saw sitting near the water two figures
        very different — one of youthful feature, naked, all his
        flesh fine, soft and supple — and the other, an old man
        robed and bearded, with skin so wrinkled rolling
        hills recall the surface of his face —

Aion and Chronos —
                in the flesh.

        Chronos cleared his throat and began to speak in a
                form of mumbling,

"Well, who is it that we have here?
Someone
wandering all the way up
here, long journey, though
a lot to see, I hope you
kept each detail in your
memory, saving each
beauty for a later date
instead of filling up your
mind simply with the
memory of the hardship
of the climb ..."

    Aion smiled, frowned, then shook his head,
"Ah, the specifics matter little,
there be plenty of time for
all the little things the
couple times around —
maybe the fourth time
around — say — isn't that a
tune? I don't remember
right ..."

Dionysus smiled at the two immortals —
sure he had heard a good many stories about the pair
when he was young, but never did he realize each
and every detail had been true, and just like time,
they rambled on ...

"The name be Dionysus, and it's likely Aion may have some
recollection of me, however faint ...
"I've come to ask the possibility of a bargain, an exchange of
time in attempts to correct the fates — for you see
I have meddled with the motions of the currents and
so have done wrong
through it ..."

    Aion was the first to answer, and his words came in
form of an interruption,
"Yesh, young one,"
the youthful looking fellow smiled,

"You know you ask a lot, for you
 work on different rules
 than the rest—or at least
 the most ...
"That being said, it sounds as
 though you'd have to
 strike a deal with the both
 of us, which I guarantee
 will turn out badly for you
 yourself,
 you see ..."

The three spoke long into the night—or so it seemed, though
 it was certainly hard to tell in a place where time flowed
 from a fountain fed from source suspended, invisible
 to the eye ...

XVII. : Eternal Recurrence

 Dionysus did not return to the city that evening,
 instead he wandered along the beach to where the
 cliffs overhung the rolling sea and waves crashed on
 the rocks so far below.

 He stared down at the water and sadly sighed aloud, the waves
 seemed cyclical as they rolled in, as if it were a never-
 ending loop, an eternal recurrence which changed
 only when the rocks eroded, and eventually the
 scenery shifted, after seemingly infinite cycles of the
 same thing ...

 Fitting then, for it was an echo of the deal made with the two
 above—an ouroboros type of misery for he, and a
 lack of meddling by he for she ...

  All happenings would be forgotten, and the cycle
   would restart—and though all would lose
   their memories, it would not be the same for
   he, and forever he would remember the loss
   of his
   Ariadne ...

And though he knew she would remember nothing,

> in the sky he placed the corona
> crafted from the poem and pen
> given long ago—for even if this
> time around she left on the ship
> with black sails, Dionysus' love
> would oversee her, laced
> high above her head ...

Standing on the overhang,
    he dove into the sea,

        and dissipated,

                like ashes scattering ...

Willows, Women, Highways and the Sea
A Book of Poems

featuring...

Song of the Corona Borealis
A Pocket Epic

has been a production of...

M.A.M. PUBLISHING

contact at
m.a.m.publishing@gmail.com

www.ingramcontent.com/pod-product-compliance
Lightning Source LLC
Chambersburg PA
CBHW022114040426
42450CB00006B/691